# Sam goes to school

**Story by Jenny Giles**
**Illustrations by Pat Reynolds**

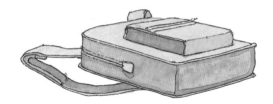

"I am going to school today,"
said Sam.

"You are a big girl, Sam,"
said Mom,
"and you can go to school."

Sam said,

"Mom, will you come into school with me?"

"Come on, Sam," said Mom.
"We will go and see the teacher."

Sam looked at the teacher.

She looked at the girls and boys.

Sam said, "Mom…

will you stay here with me?"

The teacher said,
"Sam, come and sit here
with the girls and boys."

Sam stayed with Mom.

A little girl said,

"I will look after you, Sam.

Come and sit with me."

Sam looked at the little girl,
and she looked at Mom.

Sam went with the little girl.

"Goodbye, Sam," said Mom.

"I'm going home."

"Goodbye, Mom," said Sam.

"I am a big school girl."